What the
BIBLE
Says
about
GOD'S WILL

What the
BIBLE
Says
about
GOD'S WILL

BARBOUR
PUBLISHING

ISBN 978-1-60260-279-3

Published by Barbour Publishing, Inc., P.O. Box 719, Uhrichsville, Ohio 44683, www.barbourbooks.com

Our mission is to publish and distribute inspirational products offering exceptional value and biblical encouragement to the masses.

Member of the
Evangelical Christian
Publishers Association

Printed in the United States of America

CONTENTS

INTRODUCTION:
FINDING GOD'S WILL

The Bible has more to say about finding God's will than you may realize.

To begin with, the Bible reveals God's universal will for His people. What that means is that God clearly outlines the steps He wants us to take in regard to our spiritual lives and character. In many places, the Bible plainly speaks of God's will for us on a variety of subjects such as money, honesty, and sex.

While God's will in these universal areas is unmistakable, many people seek God's specific guidance on other unique questions that may not seem to have the same clear answers: Which job should I take? Who should I marry? Where should I live?

Even when it comes to these individualized

questions, the Bible does not disappoint. In its pages you will find practical wisdom to guide you in making decisions and finding God's unique plan for your life.

CHAPTER 1

GOD'S WILL AND HIS PROMISES TO YOU

God has never left me in the dark. There have been times I've changed jobs—even moved clear across the country—but I've always sensed His presence and peace while making each decision. Through the years I've learned that God is real, He cares for me, and that He really does have a plan for my life. There's never been a day that I've doubted that He's leading me along that path in His perfect timing.

■ James, age 57, North Carolina ■

CREATING YOU WITH A PURPOSE

■ "For I know the plans I have for you," declares the LORD, "plans to prosper you and not to harm you, plans to give you hope and a future."

JEREMIAH 29:11 NIV

■ "They are my people—
I created each of them
to bring honor to me."

ISAIAH 43:7 CEV

■ However, as it is written:
"No eye has seen,
no ear has heard,
no mind has conceived
what God has prepared for those
who love him."

1 CORINTHIANS 2:9 NIV

■ It's in Christ that we find out who we are and what we are living for. Long before we first heard of Christ and got our hopes up, he had his eye on us, had designs on us for glorious living, part of the overall purpose he is working out in everything and everyone.

EPHESIANS 1:11–12 MSG

REVEALING HIS WILL

■ Therefore do not be foolish, but understand what the Lord's will is.

EPHESIANS 5:17 NIV

■ And he said, "The God of our fathers appointed you to know his will, to see the Righteous One and to hear a voice from his mouth."

ACTS 22:14 ESV

■ And so, from the day we heard, we have not ceased to pray for you, asking that you may be filled with the knowledge of his will in all spiritual wisdom and understanding.

COLOSSIANS 1:9 ESV

■ You've done all this not because of who I am but because of who you are—out of your very heart!—but you've let me in on it.

2 SAMUEL 7:21 MSG

■ You explain deep mysteries,
   because even the dark is light to you.

DANIEL 2:22 CEV

■ And he made known to us the mystery of his
   will according to his good pleasure, which he
   purposed in Christ.

EPHESIANS 1:9 NIV

■ "The secret things belong to the LORD our
   God, but the things that are revealed belong
   to us and to our children forever, that we
   may do all the words of this law."

DEUTERONOMY 29:29 ESV

DIRECTING YOUR LIFE

■ Trust in the LORD with all your heart
and lean not on your own understanding;
in all your ways acknowledge him,
and he will make your paths straight.

PROVERBS 3:5–6 NIV

■ If any of you lacks wisdom, he should ask
God, who gives generously to all without
finding fault, and it will be given to him.

JAMES 1:5 NIV

■ "Call to me and I will answer you and tell
you great and unsearchable things you do
not know."

JEREMIAH 33:3 NIV

■ Guide me in your truth and teach me, for
you are God my Savior, and my hope is in
you all day long.

PSALM 25:5 NIV

■ For this God is our God for ever and ever;
    he will be our guide even to the end.

PSALM 48:14 NIV

■ And we know that in all things God works
  for the good of those who love him, who
  have been called according to his purpose.

ROMANS 8:28 NIV

■ "And if God cares so wonderfully for flowers
  that are here today and thrown into the fire
  tomorrow, he will certainly care for you. Why
  do you have so little faith?"

LUKE 12:28 NLT

■ If I rise on the wings of the dawn,
    if I settle on the far side of the sea,
    even there your hand will guide me,
    your right hand will hold me fast.

PSALM 139:9–10 NIV

REMAINING FAITHFUL TO YOU

■ "God did this so that men would seek him and perhaps reach out for him and find him, though he is not far from each one of us."

ACTS 17:27 NIV

■ "Praise be to the LORD, the God of my master Abraham, who has not abandoned his kindness and faithfulness to my master. As for me, the LORD has led me on the journey to the house of my master's relatives."

GENESIS 24:27 NIV

■ "I am with you and will watch over you wherever you go, and I will bring you back to this land. I will not leave you until I have done what I have promised you."

GENESIS 28:15 NIV

■ The LORD replied, "My Presence will go with
you, and I will give you rest."

EXODUS 33:14 NIV

■ Even to your old age and gray hairs I am he,
I am he who will sustain you.
I have made you and I will carry you;
I will sustain you and I will rescue you.

ISAIAH 46:4 NIV

■ He said:
"In my distress I called to the LORD,
and he answered me.
From the depths of the grave I called for help,
and you listened to my cry."

JONAH 2:2 NIV

■ Being confident of this, that he who began
a good work in you will carry it on to
completion until the day of Christ Jesus.

PHILIPPIANS 1:6 NIV

ONE MOMENT
AT A TIME
FIRST THINGS
FIRST

- **Get to know God.** If you want to hear His voice and sense His direction, you'll need to improve your relationship with God. Don't let the stress of making a decision squeeze out regular prayer and time with Him.

- **Establish God's priorities in your life.** God is concerned about spreading the gospel message and growing the members of His church into Christlikeness. While your decisions may involve jobs, money, and life partners, those decisions should not be divorced from what God is doing in the world around you.

Know your ultimate purpose. While you search for His will, don't forget that your most significant calling is to be a child of God and a member of His kingdom. That truth should stay at the top of your list while you seek guidance on less significant issues.

CHAPTER 2

GOD'S WILL AND HOW HE'S CREATED YOU TO FULFILL IT

A number of years ago I met an employment counselor who was a Christian. She taught me many things about finding God's plan and direction that have changed the way I make decisions. Through her, I learned that God is an infinite God and created a world of people with infinite possibilities. My talents and passions are as unique as yours. Together our job is to discover how He has made us and to find our roles and places in this world and in His kingdom.

■ Elizabeth, age 46, Ohio ■

LIVING SUBJECT TO YOUR CREATOR

■ But now, O Jacob, listen to the LORD who
  created you.
  O Israel, the one who formed you says,
  "Do not be afraid, for I have ransomed you.
  I have called you by name; you are mine."

  ISAIAH 43:1 NLT

■ So God created man in his own image,
  in the image of God he created him;
  male and female he created them.

  GENESIS 1:27 NIV

■ Know that the LORD is God. It is he who
  made us, and we are his; we are his people,
  the sheep of his pasture.

  PSALM 100:3 NIV

■ For the LORD, the Most High, is to be feared,
a great king over all the earth.

PSALM 47:2 ESV

■ For you created my inmost being;
you knit me together in my mother's
womb.
I praise you because I am fearfully and
wonderfully made; your works are
wonderful, I know that full well.
My frame was not hidden from you
when I was made in the secret place.
When I was woven together in the depths
of the earth, your eyes saw my unformed
body.
All the days ordained for me were written
in your book before one of them came
to be.

PSALM 139:13–16 NIV

■   When I consider your heavens,
        the work of your fingers,
the moon and the stars,
        which you have set in place,
what is man that you are mindful of him,
        the son of man that you care for him?
You made him a little lower than the
        heavenly beings and crowned him with
        glory and honor.

PSALM 8:3–5 NIV

UNDERSTANDING YOUR GOD-GIVEN IDENTITY

■ You were bought at a price. Therefore honor God with your body.

1 CORINTHIANS 6:20 NIV

■ See how very much our Father loves us, for he calls us his children, and that is what we are!

1 JOHN 3:1 NLT

■ For all who are led by the Spirit of God are children of God.

So you have not received a spirit that makes you fearful slaves. Instead, you received God's Spirit when he adopted you as his own children. Now we call him, "Abba, Father."

ROMANS 8:14–15 NLT

■ I no longer call you servants, because a servant does not know his master's business. Instead, I have called you friends, for everything that I learned from my Father I have made known to you.

JOHN 15:15 NIV

■ Praise the God and Father of our Lord Jesus Christ for the spiritual blessings that Christ has brought us from heaven! Before the world was created, God had Christ choose us to live with him and to be his holy and innocent and loving people. God was kind and decided that Christ would choose us to be God's own adopted children. God was very kind to us because of the Son he dearly loves, and so we should praise God.

EPHESIANS 1:3–6 CEV

■ But to all who did receive him, who believed in his name, he gave the right to become children of God.

JOHN 1:12 ESV

■ You belong to God, so keep away from all these evil things. Try your best to please God and to be like him. Be faithful, loving, dependable, and gentle.

1 TIMOTHY 6:11 CEV

■ If someone claims, "I know God," but doesn't obey God's commandments, that person is a liar and is not living in the truth.

1 JOHN 2:4 NLT

DISCOVERING YOUR GIFTS AND TALENTS

■ These are the gifts Christ gave to the church: the apostles, the prophets, the evangelists, and the pastors and teachers. Their responsibility is to equip God's people to do his work and build up the church, the body of Christ.

EPHESIANS 4:11–12 NLT

■ There are different kinds of gifts, but the same Spirit. There are different kinds of service, but the same Lord. There are different kinds of working, but the same God works all of them in all men.

Now to each one the manifestation of the Spirit is given for the common good.

1 CORINTHIANS 12:4–7 NIV

■ All these gifts have a common origin, but are handed out one by one by the one Spirit of God. He decides who gets what, and when.

1 CORINTHIANS 12:11 MSG

■ Just as our bodies have many parts and each part has a special function, so it is with Christ's body. We are many parts of one body, and we all belong to each other.

In his grace, God has given us different gifts for doing certain things well. So if God has given you the ability to prophesy, speak out with as much faith as God has given you. If your gift is serving others, serve them well. If you are a teacher, teach well. If your gift is to encourage others, be encouraging. If it is giving, give generously. If God has given you leadership ability, take the responsibility seriously. And if you have a gift for showing kindness to others, do it gladly.

ROMANS 12:4–8 NLT

■ This is to my Father's glory, that you bear much fruit, showing yourselves to be my disciples.

JOHN 15:8 NIV

BEING GOOD STEWARDS

■ Moreover, it is required of stewards that they be found trustworthy.

1 Corinthians 4:2 esv

■ Each one should use whatever gift he has received to serve others, faithfully administering God's grace in its various forms.

1 Peter 4:10 niv

■ You put us in charge of your handcrafted
   world, repeated to us your Genesis-charge,
Made us lords of sheep and cattle,
   even animals out in the wild,
Birds flying and fish swimming,
   whales singing in the ocean deeps.
God, brilliant Lord, your name echoes around
   the world.

Psalm 8:6–9 msg

■ And the Lord said, "Who then is the faithful and wise manager, whom his master will set over his household, to give them their portion of food at the proper time? Blessed is that servant whom his master will find so doing when he comes."

LUKE 12:42–43 ESV

■ "Again, the Kingdom of Heaven can be illustrated by the story of a man going on a long trip. He called together his servants and entrusted his money to them while he was gone. He gave five bags of silver to one, two bags of silver to another, and one bag of silver to the last—dividing it in proportion to their abilities. He then left on his trip.

"The servant who received the five bags of silver began to invest the money and earned five more. The servant with two bags of silver also went to work and earned two more. But the servant who received the one bag of silver dug a hole in the ground and hid the master's money.

"After a long time their master returned from his trip and called them to give an account of how they had used his money. The servant to whom he had entrusted the five bags of silver came forward with five more and said, 'Master, you gave me five bags of silver to invest, and I have earned five more.'

"The master was full of praise. 'Well done, my good and faithful servant. You have been faithful in handling this small amount, so now I will give you many more responsibilities. Let's celebrate together!'

"The servant who had received the two bags of silver came forward and said, 'Master, you gave me two bags of silver to invest, and I have earned two more.'

"The master said, 'Well done, my good and faithful servant. You have been faithful in handling this small amount, so now I will give you many more responsibilities. Let's celebrate together!'

"Then the servant with the one bag of silver came and said, 'Master, I knew you were a harsh man, harvesting crops you didn't plant and gathering crops you didn't cultivate. I was afraid I would lose your money, so I hid it in the earth. Look, here is your money back.'

"But the master replied, 'You wicked and lazy servant! If you knew I harvested crops I didn't plant and gathered crops I didn't cultivate, why didn't you deposit my money in the bank? At least I could have gotten some interest on it.'

"Then he ordered, 'Take the money from this servant, and give it to the one with the ten bags of silver. To those who use well what they are given, even more will be given, and they will have an abundance. But from those who do nothing, even what little they have will be taken away.'"

MATTHEW 25:14–29 NLT

SUBMITTING TO GOD'S WILL

■ Submit to God and be at peace with him;
in this way prosperity will come to you.

JOB 22:21 NIV

■ And they did not do as we expected, but
they gave themselves first to the Lord and
then to us in keeping with God's will.

2 CORINTHIANS 8:5 NIV

■ "For whoever does the will of my Father in
heaven is my brother and sister and mother."

MATTHEW 12:50 NIV

■ "Now make confession to the LORD, the God
of your fathers, and do his will."

EZRA 10:11 NIV

■ "Not everyone who says to Me, 'Lord, Lord,'
will enter the kingdom of heaven, but he who
does the will of My Father who is in heaven
will enter."

MATTHEW 7:21 NASB

■ You are free to use whatever is left over from
the silver and gold for what you and your
brothers decide is in keeping with the will of
your God.

EZRA 7:18 MSG

■ The world and its desires pass away,
but the man who does the will of God
lives forever.

1 JOHN 2:17 NIV

IDENTIFYING YOUR GOD-GIVEN PASSIONS

■ The LORD gave me this message:

"I knew you before I formed you in your mother's womb.

Before you were born I set you apart and appointed you as my prophet to the nations."

JEREMIAH 1:4–5 NLT

■ For we are God's workmanship, created in Christ Jesus to do good works, which God prepared in advance for us to do.

EPHESIANS 2:10 NIV

■ Do what the LORD wants, and he will give you your heart's desire.

Let the LORD lead you and trust him to help.

PSALM 37:4–5 CEV

ONE MOMENT
AT A TIME
KNOWING HIM

- **Learn more about God's character.** As you get to know Him, you'll discover that God's plan for your life will never contradict His character. For example, He'll never lead you to a job that requires you to avoid taxes, because God is a God of integrity. He'll never lead you to leave your spouse and run off with a coworker, because God is a God of commitment and purity. Get to know Him better and His plan will become clearer.

- **Discover who you are.** Make a list of your gifts, talents, and the things you are passionate about. Once you have your list, invite a close friend or family member to make their list about you as well. Their outside opinion may

help you formulate a more objective assess-
ment of your best strengths.

■ **Be a good steward.** We often think of steward-
ship in terms of money, but our responsibility
goes well beyond dollars and cents. Are you
getting good returns on the gifts and talents
God has given you?

CHAPTER 3

GOD'S WILL CAN BE FOUND

In hindsight, I should not have been surprised that my fiancé and I broke up. The truth is, we should never have been engaged to begin with. My friends, my parents, and my sister tried to tell me, but I stubbornly refused to listen. I was too busy struggling to hold the relationship together in any way I could—including sex. Blinded by my emotions, it took me a long time to see that this relationship would never work.

■ Amber, age 28, California ■

SURRENDERING TO GOD'S PLAN

■ Look here, you who say, "Today or tomorrow we are going to a certain town and will stay there a year. We will do business there and make a profit." How do you know what your life will be like tomorrow? Your life is like the morning fog—it's here a little while, then it's gone. What you ought to say is, "If the Lord wants us to, we will live and do this or that." Otherwise you are boasting about your own plans, and all such boasting is evil.

JAMES 4:13–16 NLT

■ "I desire to do your will, O my God;
    your law is within my heart."

PSALM 40:8 NIV

■ "May your will be done on earth,
    as it is in heaven."

MATTHEW 6:10 NLT

■ But as he left, he promised, "I will come back if it is God's will." Then he set sail from Ephesus.

ACTS 18:21 NIV

■ But I will come to you very soon, if the Lord is willing, and then I will find out not only how these arrogant people are talking, but what power they have.

1 CORINTHIANS 4:19 NIV

■ "I didn't come from heaven to do what I want! I came to do what the Father wants me to do. He sent me."

JOHN 6:38 CEV

■ [Jesus prayed,] "Father, remove this cup from me. But please, not what I want. What do you want?"

LUKE 22:42 MSG

ACKNOWLEDGING THE SUPREMACY OF GOD'S PLAN

■ "Jesus must become more important,
    while I become less important."

JOHN 3:30 CEV

■ I make known the end from the beginning,
    from ancient times, what is still to come.
I say: My purpose will stand,
    and I will do all that I please.

ISAIAH 46:10 NIV

■ Whatever the LORD pleases, he does,
    in heaven and on earth,
    in the seas and all deeps.

PSALM 135:6 ESV

■ "But he stands alone, and who can oppose him?
He does whatever he pleases."

JOB 23:13 NIV

■ God always does what he plans, and that's
why he appointed Christ to choose us.

EPHESIANS 1:11 CEV

■ For God is working in you, giving you the
desire and the power to do what pleases
him.

PHILIPPIANS 2:13 NLT

■ All the peoples of the earth
    are regarded as nothing.
He does as he pleases
    with the powers of heaven
    and the peoples of the earth.
No one can hold back his hand
    or say to him: "What have you done?"

DANIEL 4:35 NIV

■ But Joseph said to them, "Don't be afraid.
Am I in the place of God? You intended to
harm me, but God intended it for good to
accomplish what is now being done, the
saving of many lives."

GENESIS 50:19–20 NIV

■ So will the words that come out of my
mouth not come back empty-handed.
They'll do the work I sent them to do,
they'll complete the assignment I gave
them.

ISAIAH 55:11 MSG

■ In his heart a man plans his course,
but the LORD determines his steps.

PROVERBS 16:9 NIV

■ Many are the plans in a man's heart,
but it is the LORD's purpose that prevails.

PROVERBS 19:21 NIV

SEEKING DIRECTION THROUGH PRAYER

◼ Lead me in the right path, O LORD,
>   or my enemies will conquer me.
> Make your way plain for me to follow.

>> PSALM 5:8 NLT

◼ Please, LORD, please save us.
>   Please, LORD, please give us success.

>> PSALM 118:25 NLT

◼ Since you are my rock and my fortress,
>   for the sake of your name lead and
>   guide me.

>> PSALM 31:3 NIV

◼ Send forth your light and your truth,
>   let them guide me;
> let them bring me to your holy mountain,
>   to the place where you dwell.

>> PSALM 43:3 NIV

■   God, listen to me shout,
        bend an ear to my prayer.
    When I'm far from anywhere,
        down to my last gasp,
    I call out, "Guide me up High
        Rock Mountain!"

PSALM 61:1–2 MSG

PRAYING YOUR DREAMS LINE UP WITH HIS WILL

■ "This, then, is how you should pray:
  'Our Father in heaven, hallowed be your
  name, your kingdom come, your will be
  done on earth as it is in heaven.'"

  MATTHEW 6:9–10 NIV

■ And how bold and free we then become in
  his presence, freely asking according to his
  will, sure that he's listening.

  1 JOHN 5:14 MSG

■ For God is my witness, whom I serve with
  my spirit in the gospel of his Son, that
  without ceasing I mention you always in my
  prayers, asking that somehow by God's will
  I may now at last succeed in coming to you.

  ROMANS 1:9–10 ESV

■ LORD, we show our trust in you by obeying your laws; our heart's desire is to glorify your name.

ISAIAH 26:8 NLT

■ I appeal to you, brothers, by our Lord Jesus Christ and by the love of the Spirit, to strive together with me in your prayers to God on my behalf, that I may be delivered from the unbelievers in Judea, and that my service for Jerusalem may be acceptable to the saints, so that by God's will I may come to you with joy and be refreshed in your company.

ROMANS 15:30–32 ESV

■ Likewise the Spirit helps us in our weakness. For we do not know what to pray for as we ought, but the Spirit himself intercedes for us with groanings too deep for words. And he who searches hearts knows what is the mind of the Spirit, because the Spirit intercedes for the saints according to the will of God.

ROMANS 8:26–27 ESV

CONFESSING THE SIN WHICH OBSCURES YOUR VIEW

■ If I had cherished sin in my heart,
   the Lord would not have listened.

PSALM 66:18 NIV

■ "We know that God does not hear sinners;
but if anyone is God-fearing and does His will,
He hears him."

JOHN 9:31 NASB

■ There's nothing wrong with God; the wrong
   is in you.
Your wrongheaded lives caused the split
   between you and God.
Your sins got between you so that he
   doesn't hear.

ISAIAH 59:2 MSG

■ Who may ascend into the hill of the LORD?
And who may stand in His holy place?
He who has clean hands and a pure heart,
Who has not lifted up his soul to falsehood
And has not sworn deceitfully.
He shall receive a blessing from the LORD
And righteousness from the God of his
   salvation.

PSALM 24:3–5 NASB

■ The LORD detests the sacrifice of the wicked,
   but he delights in the prayers of the
   upright.

PROVERBS 15:8 NLT

■ The Lord watches over everyone who
   obeys him, and he listens to their prayers.
But he opposes everyone who does evil.

1 PETER 3:12 CEV

GOING TO THE BIBLE TO FIND HIS WILL

■ Your word is a lamp to my feet
and a light for my path.

PSALM 119:105 NIV

■ Direct my footsteps according to your word;
let no sin rule over me.

PSALM 119:133 NIV

■ I believe in your commands;
now teach me good judgment and
knowledge.
I used to wander off until you disciplined me;
but now I closely follow your word.
You are good and do only good;
teach me your decrees.

PSALM 119:66–68 NLT

■ All Scripture is inspired by God and is useful to teach us what is true and to make us realize what is wrong in our lives. It corrects us when we are wrong and teaches us to do what is right. God uses it to prepare and equip his people to do every good work.

2 TIMOTHY 3:16–17 NLT

■ "If you abide in me, and my words abide in you, ask whatever you wish, and it will be done for you."

JOHN 15:7 ESV

■ I have hidden your word in my heart
    that I might not sin against you.
Praise be to you, O LORD;
    teach me your decrees.

PSALM 119:11–12 NIV

■ God's word is alive and working and is
sharper than a double-edged sword. It cuts all
the way into us, where the soul and the spirit
are joined, to the center of our joints and
bones. And it judges the thoughts and feelings
in our hearts.

HEBREWS 4:12 NCV

■ Happy are those who don't listen to the
wicked, who don't go where sinners go,
who don't do what evil people do. They love
the LORD's teachings, and they think about
those teachings day and night.

PSALM 1:1–2 NCV

TRUSTING GOD AND HIS PLAN

■ Why am I restless? I trust you!
And I will praise you again because you
help me.

PSALM 42:5 CEV

■ Whether you turn to the right or to the left,
your ears will hear a voice behind you, saying,
"This is the way; walk in it."

ISAIAH 30:21 NIV

■ Some trust in chariots, and some in horses,
but we trust in the name of the LORD
our God.

PSALM 20:7 ESV

■ LORD, every morning you hear my voice.
Every morning, I tell you what I need,
and I wait for your answer.

PSALM 5:3 NCV

■ The LORD is my light and my salvation;
      whom shall I fear?
   The LORD is the stronghold of my life;
      of whom shall I be afraid?

PSALM 27:1 ESV

■ Yet when you relied on the LORD,
      he delivered them into your hand.

2 CHRONICLES 16:8 NIV

■ Simon Peter answered, "Lord, there is no one
   else that we can go to!"

JOHN 6:68 CEV

■ That is why I am suffering here in prison. But
   I am not ashamed of it, for I know the one in
   whom I trust, and I am sure that he is able to
   guard what I have entrusted to him until the
   day of his return.

2 TIMOTHY 1:12 NLT

■ "Do not let your hearts be troubled.
Trust in God; trust also in me."

JOHN 14:1 NIV

LISTENING TO GOOD ADVICE

■ Pay attention to advice and accept correction, so you can live sensibly.

PROVERBS 19:20 CEV

■ Timely advice is lovely,
   like golden apples in a silver basket.
To one who listens, valid criticism
   is like a gold earring or other gold jewelry.

PROVERBS 25:11–12 NLT

■ Fools are headstrong and do what they like;
   wise people take advice.

PROVERBS 12:15 MSG

■ Without good advice everything goes wrong—it takes careful planning for things to go right.

PROVERBS 15:22 CEV

■ For lack of guidance a nation falls,
but many advisers make victory sure.

PROVERBS 11:14 NIV

ACQUIRING WISDOM

■ But the wisdom from above is first of all
pure. It is also peace loving, gentle at all
times, and willing to yield to others. It is
full of mercy and good deeds. It shows no
favoritism and is always sincere.

JAMES 3:17 NLT

■ God's kingdom isn't about eating and drink-
ing. It is about pleasing God, about living in
peace, and about true happiness. All this
comes from the Holy Spirit.

ROMANS 14:17 CEV

■ Fear of the LORD is the foundation of wisdom.
Knowledge of the Holy One results in good
judgment.

PROVERBS 9:10 NLT

■ To the Jews who had believed him, Jesus said, "If you hold to my teaching, you are really my disciples. Then you will know the truth, and the truth will set you free."

JOHN 8:31–32 NIV

■ The fear of the LORD is the beginning of
   wisdom; all those who practice it have
   a good understanding.
His praise endures forever!

PSALM 111:10 ESV

■ Buy the truth and do not sell it;
   get wisdom, discipline and understanding.

PROVERBS 23:23 NIV

BEING FAITHFUL IN ALL THINGS

■ "Whoever can be trusted with very little can also be trusted with much, and whoever is dishonest with very little will also be dishonest with much."

LUKE 16:10 NIV

■ "If you have raced with men on foot
and they have worn you out,
how can you compete with horses?
If you stumble in safe country,
how will you manage in the thickets by
the Jordan?"

JEREMIAH 12:5 NIV

■ If you fall to pieces in a crisis,
there wasn't much to you in the first place.

PROVERBS 24:10 MSG

■ "Yes," the king replied, "and to those who use well what they are given, even more will be given. But from those who do nothing, even what little they have will be taken away."

LUKE 19:26 NLT

■ Yes, each of us will give a personal account to God.

ROMANS 14:12 NLT

■ Barnabas wanted to take John along, the John nicknamed Mark. But Paul wouldn't have him; he wasn't about to take along a quitter who, as soon as the going got tough, had jumped ship on them in Pamphylia.

ACTS 15:37–38 MSG

■ "Then the King will say to those on his right, 'Come, you who are blessed by my Father; take your inheritance, the kingdom prepared for you since the creation of the world. For I was hungry and you gave me something to eat, I was thirsty and you gave me something to drink, I was a stranger and you invited me in, I needed clothes and you clothed me, I was sick and you looked after me, I was in prison and you came to visit me.' . . .

"The King will reply, 'I tell you the truth, whatever you did for one of the least of these brothers of mine, you did for me.'"

MATTHEW 25:34–40 NIV

FINDING PEACE WHILE YOU WAIT

■ You will keep in perfect peace him whose mind is steadfast, because he trusts in you.

ISAIAH 26:3 NIV

■ "Peace I leave with you; My peace I give to you; not as the world gives do I give to you. Do not let your heart be troubled, nor let it be fearful."

JOHN 14:27 NASB

■ "I have told you all this so that you may have peace in me. Here on earth you will have many trials and sorrows. But take heart, because I have overcome the world."

JOHN 16:33 NLT

■ I pray that God will be kind to you and will let you live in perfect peace! May you keep learning more and more about God and our Lord Jesus.

2 PETER 1:2 CEV

■ The LORD bless you and keep you;
   the LORD make his face to shine upon
   you and be gracious to you;
   the LORD lift up his countenance upon
   you and give you peace.

NUMBERS 6:24–26 ESV

■ Don't worry about anything; instead, pray about everything. Tell God what you need, and thank him for all he has done. Then you will experience God's peace, which exceeds anything we can understand. His peace will guard your hearts and minds as you live in Christ Jesus.

PHILIPPIANS 4:6–7 NLT

ONE MOMENT
AT A TIME

EXPLORING ALL
ANGLES

- **Ask God first.** The Bible reminds us to bring our requests to God. But when you do this, you also need to remember that you may receive an answer that you don't like. And while that may be difficult to swallow at first, remember that God has your entire life in His view, and He really does know what's best for you.

- **Get good advice.** Our emotions can hinder us from making good choices. While you may feel excited about an opportunity or flattered by someone who wants you to take an assignment, get objective advice from level-headed people you can trust.

Be patient. An old proverb, "Fools jump in where angels fear to tread," is often true. An opportunity that seems too good to pass up at the moment could turn out to be a mistake that you'll regret for years to come. Take your time, pray about it, and get advice before making a big decision.

CHAPTER 4

GOD'S WILL REGARDING YOUR SPIRITUAL LIFE

I've been consumed with trying to find God's plan for my life in the last few years. I've felt overwhelmed with trying to answer the big, life-changing questions on the forefront of my mind: Who am I supposed to marry? Should I go to grad school? Which job should I take? Recently, I realized that I've neglected my most important calling— developing my relationship with my heavenly Father. What's God's ultimate will for my life? To put it simply, it's to love God and know Him better.

■ Justin, age 23, Massachusetts ■

LOVING GOD

■ Love the LORD your God with all your heart and with all your soul and with all your strength.

DEUTERONOMY 6:5 NIV

■ "Now, vigilantly guard your souls: Love God, your God."

JOSHUA 23:11 MSG

■ What does the LORD your God want from you? The LORD wants you to respect and follow him, to love and serve him with all your heart and soul.

DEUTERONOMY 10:12 CEV

■ Know therefore that the LORD your God is God; he is the faithful God, keeping his covenant of love to a thousand generations of those who love him and keep his commands.

DEUTERONOMY 7:9 NIV

■ Love the LORD your God and keep his requirements, his decrees, his laws and his commands always.

DEUTERONOMY 11:1 NIV

■ "No one can serve two masters. For you will hate one and love the other; you will be devoted to one and despise the other. You cannot serve both God and money."

LUKE 16:13 NLT

■ That's right. If you diligently keep all this com-mandment that I command you to obey— love God, your God, do what he tells you, stick close to him—God on his part will drive out all these nations that stand in your way. Yes, he'll drive out nations much bigger and stronger than you.

DEUTERONOMY 11:22–23 MSG

OBEYING GOD'S COMMANDS

■ The LORD commanded us to obey all these decrees and to fear the LORD our God, so that we might always prosper and be kept alive, as is the case today.

DEUTERONOMY 6:24 NIV

■ Teach me your decrees, O LORD;
    I will keep them to the end.
Give me understanding and I will obey your
    instructions;
I will put them into practice with all my heart.

PSALM 119:33–34 NLT

■ It is the LORD your God you must follow, and him you must revere. Keep his commands and obey him; serve him and hold fast to him.

DEUTERONOMY 13:4 NIV

■ How can a young person stay pure?
    By obeying your word.
I have tried hard to find you—
    don't let me wander from your commands.
I have hidden your word in my heart,
    that I might not sin against you.

PSALM 119:9–11 NLT

■ God's readiness to give and forgive is now
public. Salvation's available for everyone!
We're being shown how to turn our backs
on a godless, indulgent life, and how to take
on a God-filled, God-honoring life. This new
life is starting right now, and is whetting our
appetites for the glorious day when our great
God and Savior, Jesus Christ, appears. He
offered himself as a sacrifice to free us from
a dark, rebellious life into this good, pure
life, making us a people he can be proud of,
energetic in goodness.

TITUS 2:11–14 MSG

■ When God is angry, money won't help you.
Obeying God is the only way to be saved
from death.

PROVERBS 11:4 CEV

MAINTAINING INTIMACY WITH GOD

■ He has showed you, O man, what is good.
And what does the LORD require of you?
To act justly and to love mercy and to walk
humbly with your God.

MICAH 6:8 NIV

■ The LORD is near to all who call on him,
    to all who call on him in truth.

PSALM 145:18 NIV

■ "What good will it be for a man if he
gains the whole world, yet forfeits his soul?
Or what can a man give in exchange for his
soul?"

MATTHEW 16:26 NIV

■ Come near to God, and God will come near to you. You sinners, clean sin out of your lives. You who are trying to follow God and the world at the same time, make your thinking pure.

JAMES 4:8 NCV

■ Seek the LORD while He may be found;
Call upon Him while He is near.

ISAIAH 55:6 NASB

■ Better is one day in your courts than a thousand elsewhere; I would rather be a doorkeeper in the house of my God than dwell in the tents of the wicked.

PSALM 84:10 NIV

■ "Yes, I am the vine; you are the branches. Those who remain in me, and I in them, will produce much fruit. For apart from me you can do nothing."

JOHN 15:5 NLT

■ You know me inside and out, you hold me together, you never fail to stand me tall in your presence so I can look you in the eye.

PSALM 41:12 MSG

CONTINUING TO GROW

■ It is God's will that you should be sanctified.

1 THESSALONIANS 4:3 NIV

■ But you, dear friends, carefully build yourselves up in this most holy faith by praying
in the Holy Spirit.

JUDE 20 MSG

■ Like newborn babies, you must crave pure
spiritual milk so that you will grow into a
full experience of salvation. Cry out for this
nourishment, now that you have had a taste
of the Lord's kindness.

1 PETER 2:2–3 NLT

■ Teach me to do Your will,
For You are my God;
Your Spirit is good.
Lead me in the land of uprightness.

PSALM 143:10 NKJV

■ Show me your ways, O LORD,
　　teach me your paths.

PSALM 25:4 NIV

■ Do your best to improve your faith. You can
　do this by adding goodness, understanding,
　self-control, patience, devotion to God, con-
　cern for others, and love. If you keep growing
　in this way, it will show that what you know
　about our Lord Jesus Christ has made your
　lives useful and meaningful. But if you don't
　grow, you are like someone who is near-
　sighted or blind, and you have forgotten that
　your past sins are forgiven.

2 PETER 1:5 – 9 CEV

■ Therefore, my dear friends, as you have
　always obeyed—not only in my presence,
　but now much more in my absence—
　continue to work out your salvation with
　fear and trembling,

PHILIPPIANS 2:12 NIV

■ For I know that nothing good dwells in me, that is, in my flesh. For I have the desire to do what is right, but not the ability to carry it out. For I do not do the good I want, but the evil I do not want is what I keep on doing. Now if I do what I do not want, it is no longer I who do it, but sin that dwells within me.

So I find it to be a law that when I want to do right, evil lies close at hand. For I delight in the law of God, in my inner being, but I see in my members another law waging war against the law of my mind and making me captive to the law of sin that dwells in my members. Wretched man that I am! Who will deliver me from this body of death? Thanks be to God through Jesus Christ our Lord!

ROMANS 7:18–25 ESV

■ But now that you have been set free from sin and have become slaves to God, the benefit you reap leads to holiness, and the result is eternal life.

ROMANS 6:22 NIV

■ And God is able to make all grace abound to you, so that in all things at all times, having all that you need, you will abound in every good work.

2 CORINTHIANS 9:8 NIV

WHAT THE BIBLE SAYS ABOUT GOD'S WILL

PRAISING GOD

■ Give to the LORD the glory he deserves!
Bring your offering and come into his
courts.

PSALM 96:8 NLT

■ Tell everyone of every nation,
"Praise the glorious power of the LORD.
He is wonderful! Praise him
and bring an offering into his temple.
Worship the LORD, majestic and holy."

1 CHRONICLES 16:28–29 CEV

■ Oh, magnify the LORD with me,
and let us exalt his name together!

PSALM 34:3 ESV

■ So whether you eat or drink or whatever you
do, do it all for the glory of God.

1 CORINTHIANS 10:31 NIV

■ Let me shout God's name with a praising song,
Let me tell his greatness in a prayer of thanks.

PSALM 69:30 MSG

■ Great is the LORD and most worthy of praise;
his greatness no one can fathom.

PSALM 145:3 NIV

■ Sing to the LORD, you saints of his;
praise his holy name.

PSALM 30:4 NIV

■ Sing to God, O kingdoms of the earth,
Sing praises to the Lord.

PSALM 68:32 NASB

■ Then a voice came from the throne, saying:
"Praise our God,
    all you his servants,
you who fear him,
    both small and great!"

REVELATION 19:5 NIV

■ LORD All-Powerful, you are greater than all others. No one is like you, and you alone are God. Everything we have heard about you is true.

2 SAMUEL 7:22 CEV

■ For great is the LORD and most worthy of
    praise; he is to be feared above all gods.
For all the gods of the nations are idols,
    but the LORD made the heavens.
Splendor and majesty are before him;
    strength and glory are in his sanctuary.
Ascribe to the LORD, O families of nations,
    ascribe to the LORD glory and strength.
Ascribe to the LORD the glory due his name;
    bring an offering and come into his courts.
Worship the LORD in the splendor of his
    holiness; tremble before him, all the earth.

PSALM 96:4–9 NIV

■ Join with me in praising the wonderful name
of the LORD our God.

DEUTERONOMY 32:3 CEV

■ O LORD, our Lord,
How majestic is Your name in all the earth,
Who have displayed Your splendor above
the heavens!

PSALM 8:1 NASB

■ Oh, the depth of the riches of the wisdom
and knowledge of God!
How unsearchable his judgments,
and his paths beyond tracing out!
"Who has known the mind of the Lord?
Or who has been his counselor?"
"Who has ever given to God,
that God should repay him?"
For from him and through him and to him
are all things.
To him be the glory forever! Amen.

ROMANS 11:33–36 NIV

■ David praised the LORD in the presence of
　　the whole assembly, saying,
"Praise be to you, O LORD,
　　God of our father Israel,
　　from everlasting to everlasting.
Yours, O LORD, is the greatness and the
　　power and the glory and the majesty
　　and the splendor, for everything in heaven
　　and earth is yours.
Yours, O LORD, is the kingdom;
　　you are exalted as head over all.
Wealth and honor come from you;
　　you are the ruler of all things.
In your hands are strength and power
　　to exalt and give strength to all."

1 CHRONICLES 29:10–12 NIV

■ Lord, you have been our dwelling place
    in all generations.
Before the mountains were brought forth,
    or ever you had formed the earth and
    the world, from everlasting to everlasting
    you are God.

PSALM 90:1–2 ESV

■ O LORD, you have examined my heart
    and know everything about me.
You know when I sit down or stand up.
You know my thoughts even when I'm far away.
You see me when I travel and when I rest
    at home.
You know everything I do.
You know what I am going to say even
    before I say it, LORD.
You go before me and follow me.
You place your hand of blessing on my head.
Such knowledge is too wonderful for me,
    too great for me to understand!

PSALM 139:1–6 NLT

■ "There is no one like you, O LORD, and there is no God but you, as we have heard with our own ears."

1 CHRONICLES 17:20 NIV

TELLING OTHERS ABOUT JESUS

■ Then Jesus came to them and said, "All authority in heaven and on earth has been given to me. Therefore go and make disciples of all nations, baptizing them in the name of the Father and of the Son and of the Holy Spirit, and teaching them to obey everything I have commanded you. And surely I am with you always, to the very end of the age."

MATTHEW 28:18–20 NIV

■ He said to his disciples, "The harvest is great, but the workers are few. So pray to the Lord who is in charge of the harvest; ask him to send more workers into his fields."

MATTHEW 9:37–38 NLT

■ For God was in Christ, reconciling the world to himself, no longer counting people's sins against them. And he gave us this wonderful message of reconciliation.

2 CORINTHIANS 5:19 NLT

■ "And you must also testify about me because you have been with me from the beginning of my ministry."

JOHN 15:27 NLT

■ Has the LORD redeemed you?
    Then speak out!
Tell others he has redeemed you from
    your enemies.

PSALM 107:2 NLT

■ Pray also for me, that whenever I open my mouth, words may be given me so that I will fearlessly make known the mystery of the gospel, for which I am an ambassador in chains. Pray that I may declare it fearlessly, as I should.

EPHESIANS 6:19–20 NIV

■ So never be ashamed to tell others about our Lord.

2 TIMOTHY 1:8 NLT

■ But you are a chosen people, a royal priest-hood, a holy nation, a people belonging to God, that you may declare the praises of him who called you out of darkness into his wonderful light.

1 PETER 2:9 NIV

BEING THANKFUL

■ Give thanks to the LORD, call on his name;
   make known among the nations what
   he has done.

PSALM 105:1 NIV

■ I pray that you will be grateful to God
   for letting you have part in what he has
   promised his people in the kingdom of light.

COLOSSIANS 1:12 CEV

■ So thank God for his marvelous love,
   for his miracle mercy to the children
   he loves.

PSALM 107:31 MSG

■ Devote yourselves to prayer with an alert
   mind and a thankful heart.

COLOSSIANS 4:2 NLT

■ O give thanks to the LORD, for He is good;
For His lovingkindness is everlasting.

1 CHRONICLES 16:34 NASB

■ Now, our God, we give you thanks,
and praise your glorious name.

1 CHRONICLES 29:13 NIV

■ LORD, I thank you for answering me.
You have saved me.

PSALM 118:21 NCV

■ And whatever you do, whether in word or
deed, do it all in the name of the Lord Jesus,
giving thanks to God the Father through him.

COLOSSIANS 3:17 NIV

PRIORITIZING THE CHURCH

■ "I will build my church, and the gates of Hades will not overcome it."

MATTHEW 16:18 NIV

■ His intent was that now, through the church, the manifold wisdom of God should be made known to the rulers and authorities in the heavenly realms.

EPHESIANS 3:10 NIV

■ Christ is also the head of the church, which is his body. He is the beginning, supreme over all who rise from the dead. So he is first in everything.

COLOSSIANS 1:18 NLT

■ Let us not give up meeting together, as some are in the habit of doing, but let us encourage one another—and all the more as you see the Day approaching.

HEBREWS 10:25 NIV

■ Look after yourselves and everyone the Holy Spirit has placed in your care. Be like shepherds to God's church. It is the flock that he bought with the blood of his own Son.

ACTS 20:28 CEV

■ Christ did this, so that he would have a glorious and holy church, without faults or spots or wrinkles or any other flaws.... None of us hate our own bodies. We provide for them and take good care of them, just as Christ does for the church.

EPHESIANS 5:27, 29 CEV

ONE MOMENT
AT A TIME
YOUR MOST
IMPORTANT
CALLING

■ **Don't forget.** Don't get so distracted trying
to find God's will for your life in other areas
that you neglect the most important area of
all: knowing Him.

■ **Build the church.** Jesus clearly stated that His
mission was to build His church. Consider
how your job, activities, and relationships can
play a role in advancing God's kingdom.

Spread the word. Others who see you turn down a big raise in order to spend more time with your family or buy an older car so that you can give the extra money to a needy person will wonder why you did so. Take every opportunity to show how God's love and calling is more important than your own personal ambition, and be prepared to explain the reason for your actions to the people who are watching.

CHAPTER 5
GOD'S WILL REGARDING YOUR MONEY AND WORK

Dollar signs do not always equal God's will. About a year ago, I took a six-figure job that promised me the world. Finally, I thought, the grass would be greener on my side of the fence. The irony is that my life has gotten worse instead of better. My eyes have become more focused on sales bonuses than on my relationship with God, and I spend more time thinking about ways to grow my portfolio rather than considering ways to mentor my kids. Honestly, I think I was more content before I took this job and I'm starting to wonder if I've made a terrible mistake.

■ Tim, age 37, New Jersey ■

STEERING CLEAR FROM THE LOVE OF MONEY

■ Keep your lives free from the love of money.

HEBREWS 13:5 NIV

■ For the love of money is a root of all kinds of evil. Some people, eager for money, have wandered from the faith and pierced themselves with many griefs.

1 TIMOTHY 6:10 NIV

■ But people who long to be rich fall into temptation and are trapped by many foolish and harmful desires that plunge them into ruin and destruction.

1 TIMOTHY 6:9 NLT

■ Teach those who are rich in this world not to be proud and not to trust in their money, which is so unreliable. Their trust should be in God, who richly gives us all we need for our enjoyment.

1 TIMOTHY 6:17 NLT

■ Whoever trusts in his riches will fall,
    but the righteous will flourish like a
    green leaf.

PROVERBS 11:28 ESV

■ "Watch out! Be on your guard against all kinds of greed; a man's life does not consist in the abundance of his possessions."

LUKE 12:15 NIV

■ And if your wealth increases,
    don't make it the center of your life.

PSALM 62:10 NLT

Whoever loves money never has money
enough; whoever loves wealth is never
satisfied with his income. This too is
meaningless.

ECCLESIASTES 5:10 NIV

HONORING YOUR DEBTS AND TAXES

■ Pay all that you owe, whether it is taxes and
fees or respect and honor.

ROMANS 13:7 CEV

■ The wicked borrow and do not repay,
    but the righteous give generously.

PSALM 37:21 NIV

■ Let no debt remain outstanding, except
the continuing debt to love one another,
for he who loves his fellowman has fulfilled
the law.

ROMANS 13:8 NIV

■ Then the Pharisees met together to plot how
to trap Jesus into saying something for which
he could be arrested. They sent some of their
disciples, along with the supporters of Herod,

to meet with him. "Teacher," they said, "we know how honest you are. You teach the way of God truthfully. You are impartial and don't play favorites. Now tell us what you think about this: Is it right to pay taxes to Caesar or not?"

But Jesus knew their evil motives. "You hypocrites!" he said. "Why are you trying to trap me? Here, show me the coin used for the tax." When they handed him a Roman coin, he asked, "Whose picture and title are stamped on it?"

"Caesar's," they replied.

"Well, then," he said, "give to Caesar what belongs to Caesar, and give to God what belongs to God."

His reply amazed them, and they went away.

MATTHEW 22:15–22 NLT

REMEMBERING THE POOR

■ Religion that God our Father accepts as pure and faultless is this: to look after orphans and widows in their distress and to keep oneself from being polluted by the world.

JAMES 1:27 NIV

■ Be rich in helping others, to be extravagantly generous.

1 TIMOTHY 6:18 MSG

■ "When you give a feast, invite the poor, the crippled, the lame, and the blind. They cannot pay you back. But God will bless you and re-ward you when his people rise from death."

LUKE 14:13–14 CEV

■ He who is kind to the poor lends to the LORD, and he will reward him for what he has done.

PROVERBS 19:17 NIV

109

■ A person who gets ahead by oppressing the poor or by showering gifts on the rich will end in poverty.

PROVERBS 22:16 NLT

■ "When you are harvesting your crops and forget to bring in a bundle of grain from your field, don't go back to get it. Leave it for the foreigners, orphans, and widows. Then the LORD your God will bless you in all you do. When you beat the olives from your olive trees, don't go over the boughs twice. Leave the remaining olives for the foreigners, orphans, and widows. When you gather the grapes in your vineyard, don't glean the vines after they are picked. Leave the remaining grapes for the foreigners, orphans, and widows."

DEUTERONOMY 24:19–21 NLT

■ Cursed is anyone who denies justice to
foreigners, orphans, or widows.

DEUTERONOMY 27:19 NLT

■ Do not mistreat widows or orphans. If you
do, they will beg for my help, and I will come
to their rescue. In fact, I will get so angry that
I will kill your men and make widows of their
wives and orphans of their children.

EXODUS 22:22–24 CEV

WORKING WITH INTEGRITY

■ Whatever you do, work at it with all
your heart, as working for the Lord,
not for men.

COLOSSIANS 3:23 NIV

■ Whatever your hand finds to do, do it with
all your might, for in the grave, where you are
going, there is neither working nor planning
nor knowledge nor wisdom.

ECCLESIASTES 9:10 NIV

■ Make it your ambition to lead a quiet life, to
mind your own business and to work with
your hands, just as we told you, so that your
daily life may win the respect of outsiders
and so that you will not be dependent on
anybody.

1 THESSALONIANS 4:11–12 NIV

■ Do not steal.
   Do not deceive or cheat one another.

LEVITICUS 19:11 NLT

■ Go to work in the morning and stick to it
   until evening without watching the clock.
   You never know from moment to moment
      how your work will turn out in the end.

ECCLESIASTES 11:6 MSG

■ In the name of the Lord Jesus Christ, we command you, brothers, to keep away from every
   brother who is idle and does not live according to the teaching you received from us.

2 THESSALONIANS 3:6 NIV

■ Now we learn that some of you just loaf
   around and won't do any work, except the
   work of a busybody. So, for the sake of our
   Lord Jesus Christ, we ask and beg these people
   to settle down and start working for a living.

2 THESSALONIANS 3:11–12 CEV

PRAYING FOR SUCCESS

■ Jabez cried out to the God of Israel, "Oh, that you would bless me and enlarge my territory! Let your hand be with me, and keep me from harm so that I will be free from pain." And God granted his request.

1 CHRONICLES 4:10 NIV

■ "O Lord, let your ear be attentive to the prayer of this your servant and to the prayer of your servants who delight in revering your name. Give your servant success today by granting him favor in the presence of this man."

NEHEMIAH 1:11 NIV

■ "O LORD, God of my master, Abraham," he prayed. "Please give me success today, and show unfailing love to my master, Abraham."

GENESIS 24:12 NLT

■ Thus says the LORD, your Redeemer,
the Holy One of Israel:
"I am the LORD your God,
who teaches you to profit,
who leads you in the way you should go."

ISAIAH 48:17 ESV

ONE MOMENT
AT A TIME
KEEPING MONEY
IN ITS PLACE

- **Provide, don't obsess.** Money is good and helpful, but the love of money can kill your spiritual life and your relationships. While you need to work hard and earn money, always keep the dollars in their place.

- **Take money out of it.** When possible, evaluate decisions without thinking about money. That's not to say that you should make decisions that cause you to jump deeply into debt, but you should be keenly aware of the ways money can cloud your ability to make the best decision.

Be a good steward. While it's good to enjoy the gifts God's given you, He has not given them to you for the sole purpose of feeding your pleasures. You have a responsibility to look for ways to serve others with what you've been given.

CHAPTER 6
GOD'S WILL REGARDING SEX, MARRIAGE, AND FAMILY

When my friend told me she was having an affair with a married man, I couldn't believe it. And when she justified it by saying she knew that God wanted them to be together, my heart broke for her. I tried to tell her that nothing could be further from the truth, but she wouldn't hear it. Although her emotions were clouding her vision, I knew that the Bible is clear. God never leads us in ways that contradict His character or His Word. Sex outside of marriage is always wrong and can never be justified as part of God's plan.

■ Janet, age 50, Indiana ■

REMAINING DEVOTED TO YOUR SPOUSE

■ And this is why a man leaves father and mother and cherishes his wife. No longer two, they become "one flesh." This is a huge mystery, and I don't pretend to understand it all.

EPHESIANS 5:31–32 MSG

■ And further, submit to one another out of reverence for Christ.

For wives, this means submit to your husbands as to the Lord. For a husband is the head of his wife as Christ is the head of the church. He is the Savior of his body, the church. As the church submits to Christ, so you wives should submit to your husbands in everything.

For husbands, this means love your wives, just as Christ loved the church. He gave up his life for her.

EPHESIANS 5:21–25 NLT

■ Wives, understand and support your husbands by submitting to them in ways that honor the Master.

COLOSSIANS 3:18 MSG

■ Husbands, in the same way be considerate as you live with your wives, and treat them with respect as the weaker partner and as heirs with you of the gracious gift of life, so that nothing will hinder your prayers.

1 PETER 3:7 NIV

■ Be devoted to one another in brotherly love. Honor one another above yourselves.

ROMANS 12:10 NIV

■ If one part of our body hurts, we hurt all
over. If one part of our body is honored,
the whole body will be happy.

1 CORINTHIANS 12:26 CEV

■ Let's see how inventive we can be in encouraging love and helping out.

HEBREWS 10:24 MSG

HOLDING MARRIAGE IN HIGH REGARD

■ Do not be unequally yoked with unbelievers. For what partnership has righteousness with lawlessness? Or what fellowship has light with darkness?

2 CORINTHIANS 6:14 ESV

■ "Haven't you read the Scriptures?" Jesus replied. "They record that from the beginning 'God made them male and female.' And he said, 'This explains why a man leaves his father and mother and is joined to his wife, and the two are united into one.' Since they are no longer two but one, let no one split apart what God has joined together."

MATTHEW 19:4–6 NLT

■ Now, I will speak to the rest of you, though I do not have a direct command from the Lord. If a Christian man has a wife who is not a believer and she is willing to continue living with him, he must not leave her. And if a Christian woman has a husband who is not a believer and he is willing to continue living with her, she must not leave him. For the Christian wife brings holiness to her marriage, and the Christian husband brings holiness to his marriage. Otherwise, your children would not be holy, but now they are holy. (But if the husband or wife who isn't a believer insists on leaving, let them go. In such cases the Christian husband or wife is no longer bound to the other, for God has called you to live in peace.) Don't you wives realize that your husbands might be saved because of you? And don't you husbands realize that your wives might be saved because of you?

1 CORINTHIANS 7:12–16 NLT

■ "I hate divorce," says the LORD God of Israel.

MALACHI 2:16 NIV

■ Finishing is better than starting.
    Patience is better than pride.

ECCLESIASTES 7:8 NLT

GUARDING YOUR SEXUAL BEHAVIOR

■ Honor marriage, and guard the sacredness of sexual intimacy between wife and husband. God draws a firm line against casual and illicit sex.

HEBREWS 13:4 MSG

■ God's will is for you to be holy, so stay away from all sexual sin.

1 THESSALONIANS 4:3 NLT

■ "But I tell you that anyone who looks at a woman lustfully has already committed adultery with her in his heart."

MATTHEW 5:28 NIV

■ Instead, clothe yourself with the presence of the Lord Jesus Christ. And don't let yourself think about ways to indulge your evil desires.

ROMANS 13:14 NLT

■ Run from anything that stimulates youthful lusts. Instead, pursue righteous living, faithfulness, love, and peace. Enjoy the companionship of those who call on the Lord with pure hearts.

2 TIMOTHY 2:22 NLT

■ Flee from sexual immorality. Every other sin a person commits is outside the body, but the sexually immoral person sins against his own body.

1 CORINTHIANS 6:18 ESV

■ Let there be no sexual immorality, impurity, or greed among you. Such sins have no place among God's people.

EPHESIANS 5:3 NLT

■ The acts of the sinful nature are obvious: sexual immorality, impurity and debauchery.

GALATIANS 5:19 NIV

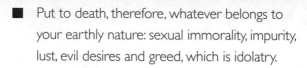

■ Put to death, therefore, whatever belongs to your earthly nature: sexual immorality, impurity, lust, evil desires and greed, which is idolatry.

COLOSSIANS 3:5 NIV

■ Because we belong to the day, we must live decent lives for all to see. Don't participate in the darkness of wild parties and drunkenness, or in sexual promiscuity and immoral living, or in quarreling and jealousy.

ROMANS 13:13 NLT

■ Do you not know that your body is a temple of the Holy Spirit, who is in you, whom you have received from God? You are not your own; you were bought at a price. Therefore honor God with your body.

1 CORINTHIANS 6:19–20 NIV

■ God has called us to live holy lives, not impure lives.

1 THESSALONIANS 4:7 NLT

RAISING YOUR CHILDREN

■ Train up a child in the way he should go;
even when he is old he will not depart
from it.

PROVERBS 22:6 ESV

■ Young people are prone to foolishness and
fads; the cure comes through tough-minded
discipline.

PROVERBS 22:15 MSG

■ Correct your children before it's too late;
if you don't punish them, you are destroying
them.

PROVERBS 19:18 CEV

■ To discipline a child produces wisdom,
but a mother is disgraced by an
undisciplined child.

PROVERBS 29:15 NLT

■ But watch out! Be careful never to forget what you yourself have seen. Do not let these memories escape from your mind as long as you live! And be sure to pass them on to your children and grandchildren. Never forget the day when you stood before the LORD your God at Mount Sinai, where he told me, "Summon the people before me, and I will personally instruct them. Then they will learn to fear me as long as they live, and they will teach their children to fear me also."

DEUTERONOMY 4:9–10 NLT

■ Fathers, do not provoke your children to anger, but bring them up in the discipline and instruction of the Lord.

EPHESIANS 6:4 ESV

■ Love GOD, your God, with your whole heart: love him with all that's in you, love him with all you've got! Write these commandments that I've given you today on your hearts. Get them inside of you and then get them inside your children. Talk about them wherever you are, sitting at home or walking in the street; talk about them from the time you get up in the morning to when you fall into bed at night. Tie them on your hands and foreheads as a reminder; inscribe them on the doorposts of your homes and on your city gates.

DEUTERONOMY 6:5–9 MSG

HONORING YOUR PARENTS

■ "Honor your father and your mother, so that you may live long in the land the LORD your God is giving you."

EXODUS 20:12 NIV

■ Grandchildren are the crowning glory of the aged; parents are the pride of their children.

PROVERBS 17:6 NLT

■ A wise child brings joy to a father;
a foolish child brings grief to a mother.

PROVERBS 10:1 NLT

■ If anyone does not provide for his relatives, and especially for his immediate family, he has denied the faith and is worse than an unbeliever.

1 TIMOTHY 5:8 NIV

■ Anyone who steals from his father and
mother and says, "What's wrong with that?"
is no better than a murderer.

PROVERBS 28:24 NLT

ONE MOMENT
AT A TIME
BE COMMITTED

- **Get to know God's purity.** God will never lead you into justifying the use of pornography or enjoying sex outside of marriage. It's simply outside His character to do so.

- **Put family first.** Focus on the needs of your family and children before focusing on the needs of your boss or employer.

- **Build your marriage.** God's will is for you to have a healthy marriage and family. This requires an ongoing investment of your time and energy. Continually look for ways to deepen your relationship with your spouse. Find ways to grow together and protect your time as a couple.

CHAPTER 7
GOD'S WILL REGARDING DEALING WITH OTHERS

Forgiving my sister for the abuse she's heaped upon me has been difficult, but God keeps making it clear to me that I need to let go of my anger. While I've felt justified in holding on to my bitterness, I've come to realize that it's contrary to God's character. If He can forgive me for the multitude of sins I've committed against Him, surely I can forgive my sister for the comparatively few sins she's committed against me.

■ Natasha, age 40, England ■

LOVING OTHERS

■ " 'Love your neighbor as yourself.'
There is no commandment greater
than these."

MARK 12:31 NIV

■ No one has ever seen God; but if we love
one another, God lives in us and his love is
made complete in us.

1 JOHN 4:12 NIV

■ Dear children, let's not merely say that we
love each other; let us show the truth by our
actions.

1 JOHN 3:18 NLT

■ If I speak in the tongues of men and of angels, but have not love, I am only a resounding gong or a clanging cymbal. If I have the gift of prophecy and can fathom all mysteries and all knowledge, and if I have a faith that can move mountains, but have not love, I am nothing. If I give all I possess to the poor and surrender my body to the flames, but have not love, I gain nothing.

Love is patient, love is kind. It does not envy, it does not boast, it is not proud. It is not rude, it is not self-seeking, it is not easily angered, it keeps no record of wrongs. Love does not delight in evil but rejoices with the truth. It always protects, always trusts, always hopes, always perseveres.

Love never fails.

1 CORINTHIANS 13:1 – 8 NIV

■ Above all, clothe yourselves with love, which binds us all together in perfect harmony. And let the peace that comes from Christ rule in your hearts. For as members of one body you are called to live in peace. And always be thankful.

COLOSSIANS 3:14–15 NLT

■ My dear friends, we must love each other. Love comes from God, and when we love each other, it shows that we have been given new life. We are now God's children, and we know him.

1 JOHN 4:7 CEV

LIVING PEACEFULLY

■ Therefore let us pursue the things which make for peace and the things by which one may edify another.

ROMANS 14:19 NKJV

■ Work at living in peace with everyone, and work at living a holy life, for those who are not holy will not see the Lord.

HEBREWS 12:14 NLT

■ Blessed are the peacemakers,
    for they will be called sons of God.

MATTHEW 5:9 NIV

■ Anyone who loves to quarrel loves sin; anyone who trusts in high walls invites disaster.

PROVERBS 17:19 NLT

BEING FREE FROM ANGER

■ Let all bitterness and wrath and anger and clamor and slander be put away from you, along with all malice.

EPHESIANS 4:31 ESV

■ In your anger do not sin: Do not let the sun go down while you are still angry.

EPHESIANS 4:26 NIV

■ Human anger does not produce the righteousness God desires.

JAMES 1:20 NLT

■ Better to be patient than powerful; better to have self-control than to conquer a city.

PROVERBS 16:32 NLT

■ But now also put these things out of your life: anger, bad temper, doing or saying things to hurt others, and using evil words when you talk.

COLOSSIANS 3:8 NCV

■ "I'm telling you that anyone who is so much as angry with a brother or sister is guilty of murder. Carelessly call a brother 'idiot!' and you just might find yourself hauled into court. Thoughtlessly yell 'stupid!' at a sister and you are on the brink of hellfire. The simple moral fact is that words kill."

MATTHEW 5:22 MSG

FORGIVING OTHERS

■ "If you forgive those who sin against you, your heavenly Father will forgive you."

MATTHEW 6:14 NLT

■ "Pay attention to yourselves! If your brother sins, rebuke him, and if he repents, forgive him, and if he sins against you seven times in the day, and turns to you seven times, saying, 'I repent,' you must forgive him."

LUKE 17:3–4 ESV

■ Be kind and compassionate to one another, forgiving each other, just as in Christ God forgave you.

EPHESIANS 4:32 NIV

■ Then Peter came to Jesus and asked, "Lord, how many times shall I forgive my brother when he sins against me? Up to seven times?"

Jesus answered, "I tell you, not seven times, but seventy-seven times."

MATTHEW 18:21–22 NIV

■ "But when you are praying, first forgive anyone you are holding a grudge against, so that your Father in heaven will forgive your sins, too."

MARK 11:25 NLT

■ God has chosen you and made you his holy people. He loves you. So you should always clothe yourselves with mercy, kindness, humility, gentleness, and patience. Bear with each other, and forgive each other. If someone does wrong to you, forgive that person because the Lord forgave you.

COLOSSIANS 3:12–13 NCV

■ "But love your enemies, do good to them, and lend to them without expecting to get anything back. Then your reward will be great, and you will be sons of the Most High, because he is kind to the ungrateful and wicked. Be merciful, just as your Father is merciful.

"Do not judge, and you will not be judged. Do not condemn, and you will not be condemned. Forgive, and you will be forgiven. Give, and it will be given to you. A good measure, pressed down, shaken together and running over, will be poured into your lap. For with the measure you use, it will be measured to you."

LUKE 6:35–38 NIV

DISCIPLING EACH OTHER

■ As iron sharpens iron, so a friend sharpens a friend.

PROVERBS 27:17 NLT

■ Guide older men into lives of temperance, dignity, and wisdom, into healthy faith, love, and endurance. Guide older women into lives of reverence so they end up as neither gossips nor drunks, but models of goodness. By looking at them, the younger women will know how to love their husbands and children, be virtuous and pure, keep a good house, be good wives. We don't want anyone looking down on God's Message because of their behavior. Also, guide the young men to live disciplined lives.

TITUS 2:2–6 MSG

■ Bear one another's burdens, and so fulfill the law of Christ.

GALATIANS 6:2 ESV

■ Therefore encourage one another and build one another up, just as you are doing.

1 THESSALONIANS 5:11 ESV

■ It's better to have a partner than go it alone.
   Share the work, share the wealth.
And if one falls down, the other helps,
   But if there's no one to help, tough!

ECCLESIASTES 4:9–10 MSG

■ My friends, we beg you to warn anyone who isn't living right. Encourage anyone who feels left out, help all who are weak, and be patient with everyone.

1 THESSALONIANS 5:14 CEV

■ You then, Timothy, my child, be strong in the grace we have in Christ Jesus. You should teach people whom you can trust the things you and many others have heard me say. Then they will be able to teach others.

2 TIMOTHY 2:1–2 NCV

ONE MOMENT
AT A TIME
LIVING AT PEACE

■ **Live peacefully.** Hebrews 12:14 reads, "Work at living in peace with everyone." While some people may be difficult to like or get along with, our call as Christians is to model peace to everyone.

■ **Look out for others.** Just as Christ came to serve and tell others about God's love and forgiveness, so we are called to represent Christ and carry that message to the world around us. Be on the lookout for ways to serve others.

Forgive. No matter how badly you've been hurt or how justified you feel in holding on to your bitterness, ask for God's help in extending forgiveness and moving on. If you choose not to forgive, bitterness will creep like a cancer into every area of your life.

CHAPTER 8

GOD'S WILL REGARDING YOUR CHARACTER

As a high school teacher at a Christian school, I enjoy working with kids who are concerned about finding God's will for their lives. Where should they go to college? Should they join the military? What career paths should they pursue? Many of them are consumed with God's plan for their futures. When they get fully worked up with these questions, I often tell them, "I can tell you with 100 percent certainty what God's plan for your life is." When they challenge me, I tell them the answer is simple: character. You want to know what God's will is for your life? It's to be a person with good character.

■ Mitch, age 43, New York ■

BEING FILLED WITH INTEGRITY

■ The integrity of the honest keeps them on track; the deviousness of crooks brings them to ruin.

PROVERBS 11:3 MSG

■ "I know, my God, that you test the heart and are pleased with integrity. All these things have I given willingly and with honest intent. And now I have seen with joy how willingly your people who are here have given to you."

1 CHRONICLES 29:17 NIV

■ "To the faithful you show yourself faithful; to those with integrity you show integrity."

2 SAMUEL 22:26 NLT

■ A good name is to be chosen rather than great riches, and favor is better than silver or gold.

PROVERBS 22:1 ESV

■ The man of integrity walks securely,
but he who takes crooked paths
will be found out.

PROVERBS 10:9 NIV

■ Better is a poor person who walks in his integrity than one who is crooked in speech and is a fool.

PROVERBS 19:1 ESV

RESISTING PRIDE

■ Pride goes before destruction,
a haughty spirit before a fall.

PROVERBS 16:18 NIV

■ Too much pride can put you to shame.
It's wiser to be humble.

PROVERBS 11:2 CEV

■ Too much pride causes trouble. Be sensible
and take advice.

PROVERBS 13:10 CEV

■ To fear the LORD is to hate evil; I hate pride and
arrogance, evil behavior and perverse speech.

PROVERBS 8:13 NIV

■ Always be humble and gentle. Be patient with
each other, making allowance for each other's
faults because of your love.

EPHESIANS 4:2 NLT

■ For by the grace given me I say to every one of you: Do not think of yourself more highly than you ought, but rather think of yourself with sober judgment, in accordance with the measure of faith God has given you.

ROMANS 12:3 NIV

■ One of Satan's angels was sent to make me suffer terribly, so that I would not feel too proud. Three times I begged the Lord to make this suffering go away. But he replied, "My kindness is all you need. My power is strongest when you are weak." So if Christ keeps giving me his power, I will gladly brag about how weak I am. Yes, I am glad to be weak or insulted or mistreated or to have troubles and sufferings, if it is for Christ. Because when I am weak, I am strong.

2 CORINTHIANS 12:7–10 CEV

■ Yes, all of you be submissive to one another,
and be clothed with humility, for "God resists
the proud, But gives grace to the humble."
Therefore humble yourselves under the
mighty hand of God, that He may exalt you
in due time.

1 PETER 5:5–6 NKJV

■ This is what the LORD says:
"The wise must not brag about their wisdom.
The strong must not brag about their
    strength.
The rich must not brag about their money.
But if people want to brag, let them brag
    that they understand and know me.
Let them brag that I am the LORD,
    and that I am kind and fair,
    and that I do things that are right on earth.
This kind of bragging pleases me," says the
    LORD.

JEREMIAH 9:23–24 NCV

OVERCOMING TEMPTATION

■ The temptations in your life are no different from what others experience. And God is faithful. He will not allow the temptation to be more than you can stand. When you are tempted, he will show you a way out so that you can endure.

1 CORINTHIANS 10:13 NLT

■ Blessed is the man who perseveres under trial, because when he has stood the test, he will receive the crown of life that God has promised to those who love him. When tempted, no one should say, "God is tempting me." For God cannot be tempted by evil, nor does he tempt anyone.

JAMES 1:12–13 NIV

■ Dear brothers and sisters, when troubles come your way, consider it an opportunity for great joy. For you know that when your faith is tested, your endurance has a chance to grow.

JAMES 1:2–3 NLT

■ Finally, brothers, whatever is true, whatever is noble, whatever is right, whatever is pure, whatever is lovely, whatever is admirable—if anything is excellent or praiseworthy—think about such things.

PHILIPPIANS 4:8 NIV

■ Those who live according to the sinful nature have their minds set on what that nature desires; but those who live in accordance with the Spirit have their minds set on what the Spirit desires.

ROMANS 8:5 NIV

■ As obedient children, do not conform to the evil desires you had when you lived in ignorance.

1 PETER 1:14 NIV

■ For the grace of God that brings salvation has appeared to all men. It teaches us to say "No" to ungodliness and worldly passions, and to live self-controlled, upright and godly lives in this present age.

TITUS 2:11–12 NIV

ONE MOMENT
AT A TIME
CHARACTER
FIRST

- **Proper focus.** Your life is not about what you do, but it's about who you are. Develop your character first and foremost.

- **You are not the ultimate end.** God did not create the universe for you, but for Him. Work on developing your character so that you honor Him and worship Him with your life.

Evaluate yourself. Take an hour on a Sunday afternoon and ask God to help you evaluate areas of your character that need refinement. Choose one specifically and explore what the Bible says about it. Ask God to help you grow in this area.

CHAPTER 9

GOD'S WILL MAY BE PAINFUL

For a long time, I wanted to be doctor. I played with the toy medical kits as a kid and went off to college as a premed student. While I did pretty well, my MCAT scores were below average. And while I've sent many applications off to med schools, each has come back with a standard rejection letter. It's becoming fairly clear that God's plan for me is not what I had hoped it would be. Saying good-bye to my dream has been difficult, but I'm slowly working through it. While it still hurts, I realize that God has other plans for me, and because they're His plans, they're better.

■ Lauren, age 26, Illinois ■

TRUSTING THROUGH THE DISAPPOINTMENT

■ Though he slay me, yet will I hope in him.

JOB 13:15 NIV

■ Listen to my cry for help, my King and my
God, for I pray to no one but you.

PSALM 5:2 NLT

■ I'll never forget the trouble, the utter lostness,
    the taste of ashes, the poison I've
    swallowed.
I remember it all—oh, how well I
    remember—the feeling of hitting
    the bottom.
But there's one other thing I remember,
    and remembering, I keep a grip on hope:
God's loyal love couldn't have run out,
    his merciful love couldn't have dried up.

LAMENTATIONS 3:19–22 MSG

■ Remember, it is better to suffer for doing good, if that is what God wants, than to suffer for doing wrong!

1 PETER 3:17 NLT

■ "You're blessed when you feel you've lost what is most dear to you. Only then can you be embraced by the One most dear to you."

MATTHEW 5:4 MSG

■ Taste and see that the LORD is good;
blessed is the man who takes refuge in him.

PSALM 34:8 NIV

■ I learned God-worship
when my pride was shattered.
Heart-shattered lives ready for love
don't for a moment escape God's notice.

PSALM 51:17 MSG

■ Do you not know?
    Have you not heard?
The LORD is the everlasting God,
    the Creator of the ends of the earth.
He will not grow tired or weary,
    and his understanding no one can fathom.
He gives strength to the weary
    and increases the power of the weak.
Even youths grow tired and weary,
    and young men stumble and fall;
but those who hope in the LORD
    will renew their strength.
They will soar on wings like eagles;
    they will run and not grow weary,
    they will walk and not be faint.

ISAIAH 40:28–31 NIV

■ Fig trees may no longer bloom, or vineyards produce grapes; olive trees may be fruitless, and harvest time a failure; sheep pens may be empty, and cattle stalls vacant—but I will still celebrate because the LORD God saves me.

The LORD gives me strength.

He makes my feet as sure as those of a deer, and he helps me stand on the mountains.

HABAKKUK 3:17–19 CEV

REFUSING TO ENVY OTHERS

■ Then I observed that most people are motivated to success because they envy their neighbors. But this, too, is meaningless—like chasing the wind.

ECCLESIASTES 4:4 NLT

■ You want what you don't have, so you scheme and kill to get it. You are jealous of what others have, but you can't get it, so you fight and wage war to take it away from them. Yet you don't have what you want because you don't ask God for it. And even when you ask, you don't get it because your motives are all wrong—you want only what will give you pleasure.

JAMES 4:2–3 NLT

■ Resentment kills a fool,
and envy slays the simple.

JOB 5:2 NIV

■ So put away all malice and all deceit and
hypocrisy and envy and all slander.

1 PETER 2:1 ESV

■ It's healthy to be content, but envy can eat
you up.

PROVERBS 14:30 CEV

SENSING GOD'S CARE WHEN DREAMS DISAPPEAR

■ The LORD is good to everyone. He showers compassion on all his creation. All of your works will thank you, LORD, and your faithful followers will praise you.

PSALM 145:9–10 NLT

■ Praise be to the God and Father of our Lord Jesus Christ, the Father of compassion and the God of all comfort, who comforts us in all our troubles, so that we can comfort those in any trouble with the comfort we ourselves have received from God. For just as the sufferings of Christ flow over into our lives, so also through Christ our comfort overflows.

2 CORINTHIANS 1:3–5 NIV

■ For the LORD your God is living among you. He is a mighty savior. He will take delight in you with gladness. With his love, he will calm all your fears. He will rejoice over you with joyful songs.

ZEPHANIAH 3:17 NLT

■ But Zion said, "I don't get it. God has left me. My Master has forgotten I even exist." [And God replied,] "Can a mother forget the infant at her breast, walk away from the baby she bore? But even if mothers forget, I'd never forget you—never. Look, I've written your names on the backs of my hands. The walls you're rebuilding are never out of my sight. Your builders are faster than your wreckers. The demolition crews are gone for good. Look up, look around, look well! See them all gathering, coming to you? As sure as I am the living God."

ISAIAH 49:14–18 MSG

■ "My covenant of blessing will never be broken," says the LORD, who has mercy on you.

ISAIAH 54:10 NLT

■ But you, O God, do see trouble and grief;
  you consider it to take it in hand.
The victim commits himself to you;
  you are the helper of the fatherless.

PSALM 10:14 NIV

■ The LORD is like a father to his children, tender and compassionate to those who fear him.

PSALM 103:13 NLT

■ Pray that our LORD will make us strong and give us peace.

PSALM 29:11 CEV

■ God, high above, sees far below;
　　no matter the distance, he knows
　　everything about us.

PSALM 138:6 MSG

■ And Solomon, my son, learn to know the
　God of your ancestors intimately. Worship
　and serve him with your whole heart and a
　willing mind. For the LORD sees every heart
　and knows every plan and thought. If you
　seek him, you will find him. But if you forsake
　him, he will reject you forever.

1 CHRONICLES 28:9 NLT

■ Give ear and come to me;
　　hear me, that your soul may live.
　I will make an everlasting covenant with you,
　　my faithful love promised to David.

ISAIAH 55:3 NIV

■ "The God who made the world and everything in it is the Lord of heaven and earth and does not live in temples built by hands. And he is not served by human hands, as if he needed anything, because he himself gives all men life and breath and everything else. From one man he made every nation of men, that they should inhabit the whole earth; and he determined the times set for them and the exact places where they should live. God did this so that men would seek him and perhaps reach out for him and find him, though he is not far from each one of us."

ACTS 17:24–27 NIV

REMAINING CONTENT

■ Keep a sharp eye out for weeds of bitter discontent. A thistle or two gone to seed can ruin a whole garden in no time.

HEBREWS 12:15 MSG

■ "So do not worry, saying, 'What shall we eat?' or 'What shall we drink?' or 'What shall we wear?' For the pagans run after all these things, and your heavenly Father knows that you need them. But seek first his kingdom and his righteousness, and all these things will be given to you as well. Therefore do not worry about tomorrow, for tomorrow will worry about itself. Each day has enough trouble of its own."

MATTHEW 6:31–34 NIV

■ But if we have food and clothing, we will be content with that.

1 TIMOTHY 6:8 NIV

■ Unless the LORD builds the house,
    its builders labor in vain. . . .
In vain you rise early
    and stay up late,
toiling for food to eat—
    for he grants sleep to those he loves.

PSALM 127:1–2 NIV

■ I know what it is to be in need, and I know what it is to have plenty. I have learned the secret of being content in any and every situation, whether well fed or hungry, whether living in plenty or in want. I can do everything through him who gives me strength.

PHILIPPIANS 4:12–13 NIV

■ Yes, we should make the most of what God gives, both the bounty and the capacity to enjoy it, accepting what's given and delighting in the work. It's God's gift!

ECCLESIASTES 5:19 MSG

ONE MOMENT
AT A TIME
FACING THE
PAIN

- **Admit the loss.** God is a caring Father who shows great compassion when the dreams of His children don't work out. You can pour out your pain to Him and know that He's listening.

- **Find contentment.** While your plans may not line up with God's plans, you are still blessed. He has given you other gifts and opportunities which are yours to enjoy. Be sure to count those blessings and thank Him for them.

Embrace God's plan. When life takes an unexpected turn, you can embrace the change or get bogged down in disappointment. Don't let God-given opportunities pass by because you're too busy holding on to the wrong things.

CHAPTER 10
GOD'S WILL MAY INVOLVE RISK

Steps of faith can be scary, but I suppose that's why they require faith. When I felt led to change jobs, I was terrified. But as I read the Bible, I realized I was in good company. People like Abraham, Moses, and David all had great callings that began with scary steps of faith. God asked each one to leave a comfortable existence and follow His direction into a life filled with challenge and risk. But each also had the satisfaction of God's approval and reward. While I don't know how my next steps will turn out, I know that God's bigger than I can imagine and He'll protect me along the way.

■ Nadia, age 42, Connecticut ■

BEING BOLD

■ If any of you lacks wisdom, he should ask God, who gives generously to all without finding fault, and it will be given to him. But when he asks, he must believe and not doubt, because he who doubts is like a wave of the sea, blown and tossed by the wind.

JAMES 1:5–6 NIV

■ Don't worry about anything; instead, pray about everything. Tell God what you need, and thank him for all he has done.

PHILIPPIANS 4:6 NLT

■ So whenever we are in need, we should come bravely before the throne of our merciful God. There we will be treated with undeserved kindness, and we will find help.

HEBREWS 4:16 CEV

■ Be brave and strong! Don't be afraid. . .The
   LORD your God will always be at your side,
   and he will never abandon you.

                                     DEUTERONOMY 31:6 CEV

■ "Have I not commanded you? Be strong and
   courageous. Do not be terrified; do not be
   discouraged, for the LORD your God will be
   with you wherever you go."

                                     JOSHUA 1:9 NIV

STEPPING OUT IN FAITH

■ Now unto him that is able to do exceeding abundantly above all that we ask or think, according to the power that worketh in us, Unto him be glory in the church by Christ Jesus throughout all ages, world without end. Amen.

EPHESIANS 3:20–21 KJV

■ May the God of peace, who through the blood of the eternal covenant brought back from the dead our Lord Jesus, that great Shepherd of the sheep, equip you with everything good for doing his will, and may he work in us what is pleasing to him, through Jesus Christ, to whom be glory for ever and ever. Amen.

HEBREWS 13:20–21 NIV

■ But grow in the grace and knowledge of our Lord and Savior Jesus Christ. To him be glory both now and forever! Amen.

2 PETER 3:18 NIV

■ By faith Abraham, when called to go to a place he would later receive as his inheritance, obeyed and went, even though he did not know where he was going.

HEBREWS 11:8 NIV

■ It's impossible to please God apart from faith. And why? Because anyone who wants to approach God must believe both that he exists and that he cares enough to respond to those who seek him.

HEBREWS 11:6 MSG

PERSEVERING TO THE END

■ But you need to stick it out, staying with God's plan so you'll be there for the promised completion.

HEBREWS 10:36 MSG

■ Be careful about the way you live and about what you teach. Keep on doing this, and you will save not only yourself, but the people who hear you.

1 TIMOTHY 4:16 CEV

■ But I don't care what happens to me, as long as I finish the work that the Lord Jesus gave me to do.

ACTS 20:24 CEV

■ To him who overcomes and does my will to the end, I will give authority over the nations.

REVELATION 2:26 NIV

■ Do you not know that in a race all the
runners run, but only one gets the prize?
Run in such a way as to get the prize.

1 CORINTHIANS 9:24 NIV

■ Epaphras, who is one of you and a servant
of Christ Jesus, sends greetings. He is always
wrestling in prayer for you, that you may
stand firm in all the will of God, mature and
fully assured.

COLOSSIANS 4:12 NIV

■ Those who live only to satisfy their own sinful
nature will harvest decay and death from that
sinful nature. But those who live to please
the Spirit will harvest everlasting life from
the Spirit. So let's not get tired of doing what
is good. At just the right time we will reap a
harvest of blessing if we don't give up.

GALATIANS 6:8–9 NLT

ONE MOMENT
AT A TIME
TAKING A RISK

■ **Seek the greatest return.** It may always feel safer to stay put, but are there greater eternal returns for your gifts if you take the next step?

■ **Called for Him.** God has called you to serve Him. It is your job to go where He leads you and to love Him with all your heart, soul, mind, and strength.

He never said it would be easy. Faith requires stepping out in trust when you may not be able to orchestrate the outcome. The Bible is filled with stories of men and women who took difficult steps of faith that led them down a long and challenging road. But because they believed in the eternal rewards at the end of their journey, they stepped out anyway. They knew it was worth it.